9/07

21

Fresh
Coat

Fresh Coat

Simple Painting Makeovers for Walls, Furniture & Fabric

Shannon Kaye

A Division of Sterling Publishing Co., Inc.
New York / London

Series Editor: Candice Janco
Assisant Editor: Matt Paden
Contributing Writer: Jess Clarke
Series Designer: Thom Gaines
Page Designer: Jackie Kerr
Cover Designer: DIY Network, Stewart Pack
Copy Editor: Jessica Boing

10 9 8 7 6 5 4 3 2 1

First Edition

Published by Lark Books, A Division of
Sterling Publishing Co., Inc.
387 Park Avenue South, New York, N.Y. 10016

Text © 2007, Lark Books
Design © 2007, Lark Books
Photography © 2007, DIY Network

Distributed in Canada by Sterling Publishing,
c/o Canadian Manda Group, 165 Dufferin Street
Toronto, Ontario, Canada M6K 3H6

Distributed in the United Kingdom by GMC Distribution Services,
Castle Place, 166 High Street, Lewes, East Sussex, England BN7 1XU

Distributed in Australia by Capricorn Link (Australia) Pty Ltd.,
P.O. Box 704, Windsor, NSW 2756 Australia

If you have questions or comments about this book, please contact:
Lark Books
67 Broadway
Asheville, NC 28801
(828) 253-0467

Manufactured in China

ISBN 13: 978-1-60059-184-6
ISBN 10: 1-60059-184-1

**For information about custom editions,
special sales, premium and corporate purchases,
please contact Sterling Special Sales Department
at 800-805-5489 or specialsales@sterlingpub.com.**

Fresh Coat **Contents**

Fresh Coat

Almost everyone at some point has looked at the plain white walls in his or her home and thought, "I wish there was some great color there." You think about a soft green or bright yellow, but not knowing where to go from there, you try to ignore it a little longer. Or maybe you've kept a piece of furniture because, though outdated, it holds fond memories. You can't let go of the furniture, but you don't want to keep hiding it either. Well, I'm glad you picked up this book because so many things can be fixed, revised, and brought back to life with a fresh coat of paint. And painting is a straightforward and cost-effective way to transform a room or favorite piece for maximum impact. A good paint job can help you sell your home, put your stamp of personality on a new space, or brighten up the walls you've stared at for years. Our homeowners have done all of that with just a few tips and tricks, and I'm excited to share these easy, time-saving ideas with you.

In the chapters ahead, you'll find all kinds of projects for bedrooms, living rooms, kitchens, and work & play rooms. But don't limit yourself to just those rooms. Painting a lamp or lampshade can brighten up any room in the house, and special finishes for wood can look luxurious on coffee tables, dressers, and cabinets alike. You can work through a set of projects in the book to recreate one of our rooms for your home, or take an idea and use it somewhere perfect for you.

The book contains basic steps and helpful techniques for you weekend warriors out there who just need to get your project done. But there's also room for adventure with decorative painting finishes that take a little practice and some unusual techniques.

Most of the tools you'll need are available in paint, home improvement, craft, and art stores. You can find some great products on the Internet and surprisingly reliable tools in your own home. I use household sponges and paper towels all the time. Fun, new gadgets are out there, too, and we explore them in the television show and book, but you'll also see that you can do a lot with a good brush and a few tips.

I love painting because it gives me a great sense of accomplishment. Every time I see that satisfied look on homeowners' faces, I know I've given them the right advice. I've called some homeowners afterward to ask if they painted anything else in their house. The answer is a resounding "Yes!" time after time. So grab a brush, flip to your favorite pages in the book, and get started. Find your inspiration, and create a space that is uniquely yours — all with just paint.

Shannon Kaye

Shannon Kaye
Host of DIY Network's *Fresh Coat*

Fresh Coat

Basics

Just like with any home improvement project, painting has a host of specialty tools, techniques, and lingo that is handy to become familiar with before taking on any project. This section supplies all of the information you'll need to buy the materials, set up the painting area, and get started without making the mistakes common to beginners. Also included are special tips that will help make any painting project easier.

Shannon

diy network

BASICS

Ready for a makeover? Whether you're painting just one room in the house or many, these tools, techniques, suggestions, and pro tips will help you get the project started right.

Before you grab your brush or roller, set up the room or environment where you'll be working. Remove furniture, household items, and anything else that will get in your way while you paint. Remove all extra pieces such as artwork, wall hangings, switch and outlet plates, and drawers, knobs, and hinges from furniture and cabinets.

Next, cover the surfaces you don't want to paint. Dropcloths effectively cover a work surface such as a table. The cloths are perfect to cover carpets and rugs, too, but be sure to spread them out completely to avoid tripping or spilling. Some surfaces, such as hardwood and tile floors, can be slippery when they're covered. Tape rosin paper over those types of surfaces to provide stability and protection. Rosin paper is a heavy, protective material available in paint and home improvement stores. It's important to use wide painter's tape to secure rosin paper.

Taping is another important step in preparation. Painter's tape, or blue tape, works well for all types of painting projects. The tape comes in levels of tackiness to ensure proper adhesion as it protects the surface it covers. Medium-tack painter's tape is a good choice, but ask a professional for recommendations for the surface you're taping. Tape off all areas you don't want painted. For rooms, this can include taping off trim from baseboards to window molding to avoid difficult touch-ups. For furniture, taping off areas you won't paint can prevent paint buildup that may make the drawers and doors hard to use.

To tape off an area you don't want to paint: Pull about eight inches of tape from the roll, and place the end on the spot where you want to start taping. Anchor that end with your free hand, and pull the roll of tape out another eight inches or so. Keep the strip close to the area you're taping.

Guiding the tape with the roll, use your free hand to place a finger about eight inches up the strip, and push down where you want the tape to go. Slide that finger back toward the anchored end to adhere the tape to the surface.

Continue pulling out tape and guiding with the hand that holds the roll and positioning and pressing with the free hand. It takes practice, but it's worth the effort. For good adhesion, after you tape use a small brush to paint just a bit of varnish along the edge of the tape where you'll be painting. That seals the tape and creates a clean line once the paint is applied. The varnish step won't seal gaps or edges that are not properly smoothed out, so take your time with both taping and sealing to ensure success.

Furniture should be raised off the floor to allow your tools and brushes to work cleanly to the bottom of the piece. Easy props include paint cans, sawhorses, or any other sturdy object that can be placed safely under the piece so the legs or sides hang freely. If the furniture is too difficult to lift, place pieces of cardboard beneath it to prevent tools and brushes from sweeping up dirt from the dropcloth as you paint.

Now check your list of supplies, and read through instructions to make sure everything you need is at your fingertips. You can prevent spills and accidents by unwrapping and placing nearby all the tools and supplies you need.

PREPARING THE SURFACE

Make sure the item you'll paint is repaired beforehand. Fill holes, replace broken pieces, and remove loose paint or paper. Be sure to sand wood furniture well to remove old paint and dirt and create a surface that will accept paint. For metals, scrape away rust and dirt, and wipe down plastics with a degreasing product. Consult with a paint professional about preparations and products for the surface you're painting. If walls have been patched, sand and prime those areas before you paint. Unprimed patches absorb paint differently than the painted area around it. The patched area will be obvious if it's painted without being primed first. For walls previously painted in any type of sheen-finish paint, wash them thoroughly with TSP (trisodium phosphate), and rinse them well to remove gloss and dirt.

Use primer on walls to prepare patches and repairs, create a surface that may be painted over wallpaper, make a mildew- and stain-resistant barrier, and neutralize the current wall color to prepare it for a new hue. Primer, which comes in multiple forms, bonds to a variety of surfaces and creates a durable surface that will accept paint. Gesso is an artist's medium that's used to prime furniture, frames, and decorative wood and plaster pieces. Gesso, a chalky, white medium available at art and craft stores, adheres strongly to wooden surfaces, including furniture, and creates a luxurious look. Prime metals, plastics, and other materials with the proper priming materials. Most of these materials will be sprays and somewhat toxic, so be sure to use them in well-ventilated areas and with proper respiratory protection. Use the same process for priming walls as you do for painting — cut in all edges and corners with the primer before you roll it on. Cutting in is using a brush to paint tight areas such as molding and corners.

Following a few simple tips will make your painting projects simpler.

Remember that it's easier to add paint than it is to take it away. A few thin, even layers always cover better than one thick, sloppy coat. For furniture, a light sanding between each coat will create a beautiful finish.

Work from inside to outside, top to bottom, and back to front to let gravity be in your favor. With a cabinet, paint the top inside piece first, then the inside back of the piece, followed by the sides and bottom. Then start at the top exterior of the piece, and work your way to the sides, followed by the front.

For rooms, always cut in the edges first. When you roll, start at one end of a wall, and work your way all the way across before you start on another wall. Use a slight "W" or "X" motion to get good coverage without striped roller marks. Roll as close to the edges of the room as possible, and go over your brush marks from cutting in to get a smooth, even finish.

Whenever possible, keep the area tidy, and allow fresh air to circulate. Wear a face mask to sand and dust, wear a respirator when you spray indoors or use toxic materials, and follow all directions for the tools and supplies.

Keep clean rags or paper towels — dry and damp — handy for accidents. And have a plastic bag available to wrap up your brush or roller during breaks or between layers.

Brushes. For best results, use larger brushes for large areas and smaller brushes for tighter spots. Angle brushes are best for painting interior trim and moldings. They come in varying widths, with the bristles cut at an angle to reach into corners. Square brushes are for cutting in walls and flat surfaces and come in a variety of sizes. Brush bristles are made in all kinds of materials and combinations, but for easy selection remember that natural bristles are for oil paints while synthetic bristles are for latex or water-based paints.

Foam brushes are for small, quick projects and great for furniture also to help avoid heavy brush marks. Artist's brushes work best for painting details. They come in a variety of shapes and sizes and often are sold in sets. Specialty brushes for decorative finishes are available at paint and home improvement stores. Stippling brushes range in size and are generally round or rectangular with a broad surface of bristles to pounce paint into a surface. Pouncing is a tapping motion that spreads the paint with each hit into a fine, spotted texture.

Brush care. Caring for brushes saves time and money in the long run. Try to dip your brush no more than 1-1 1/2 inches into the paint, and keep as much paint as possible away from the ferrule (the metal strap that holds the bristles). As soon as you're finished, rinse brushes with warm water and a little mild soap if necessary. Shake excess water out of the brush, and hang it to dry from the handle with the bristles facing down.

Glaze. Glaze is useful in many techniques but is itself a basic medium. Glaze is a transparent liquid that, when mixed with paint, colorants, or tints, becomes a translucent color. The translucent quality is determined by the amount of glaze in relation to the amount of pigment. For example, one part of glaze mixed with two parts of paint would create a near opaque finish with just a hint of transparency. Four parts of glaze mixed with one part of paint would create an almost sheer wash of color. Glaze generally stays wet longer than paint, but it's important to test a mixture on a surface to understand the rate at which that surface will absorb the glaze. It's best to paint over a low-sheen finish to allow the glaze to remain wet while you work the technique into it. Tinted glazes also are available in paint and home improvement stores.

Matte medium. Decoupage is a popular craft in which you attach paper products to a piece such as a drawer front, jewelry box, or picture frame. When brushed on each surface, matte medium acts as a glue to attach the paper to the piece and is a protective clear coat by sealing the entire surface.

Paint products. Most paint products used in this book's projects are water-based, including latex and acrylics. The products are generally less toxic, easy to clean up, and dry more quickly. Check the label to determine the base of a product. If the label says to clean up with water or soapy water, the product probably is water-based. If the label advises you to clean up with mineral spirits or any other chemical, the product probably is oil- or chemical-based, like most spray paints and stains. Follow the directions for these and all paints. As in cooking, oil and water do not mix well in painting. Though there are a few exceptions, to keep things simple use like products whenever possible.

Other water-based products in the book are matte medium, tempera, gesso, and fabric paint. You also may use glaze, varnish, extenders, and primers. These products are available in oil- or chemical-based form as well, so check the label whenever you buy products or mix mediums.

Sheen refers to the glossy quality of paint or varnish. Flat-finish paint has no sheen. Flat paint generally is easy to touch up but difficult to clean because of its dry, chalky nature. Matte-finish paint creates a finish similar to flat paint but is easier to clean. Eggshell, satin, and low-sheen finishes have a relatively low level of gloss. Semi-gloss and gloss-finish paints are used commonly for trim as well as walls in kitchens and bathrooms because the paints are durable and easy to clean, but they often create glare and discomfort in light. It's a good idea to use lower-sheen finishes for kitchens and bathrooms because those finishes are durable, easy to clean, and provide a softer finish.

Primer. For many projects, you should start with a good coat of primer. Be sure to check the labels to select the right primer for the right surface. Sprays work well on nonporous surfaces such as plastic, metal, and laminates. To get better coverage, ask your paint dealer to tint the paint for you. Primer usually can be tinted up to 50 percent of the pigment formula and still retain its coverage and adhesive qualities. The result is a mixture that will be lighter than your paint color but will cut down on the coats required for a solid, true hue.

Rollers. Basic rollers usually are 9" long and have different lengths of nap, or thickness. Shorter nap works well on smooth walls while longer nap gets into the details of more textured surfaces. Roller handles are about 18" long, but you can buy them longer or purchase extension rods to reach ceiling heights without using a ladder. The extension rods are great for painting floors. Rollers are also available in smaller, thinner shapes and are perfect for touching up walls, applying specialty finishes, and painting in tight areas.

Sponges. These handy tools are used for everything from cleanup to specialty techniques and finishes. Whatever sponge you choose, always "hide" the tool when you create special finishes. Twist and turn the sponge to manipulate the shape that covers the surface without a spotty, sponged result.

TECHNIQUES

You may choose from many decorative painting techniques. Here are common techniques used in the projects in this book. Check stores or libraries for books with more complete listings and instructions. The possibilities are endless, so don't be afraid to experiment.

Burnishing. Pressing or pushing to smooth out a surface is burnishing. The technique helps create better adhesion for tape and assists with adhesive stencils. Burnishing tools can be your thumbnail, a credit card, plastic spreader, putty knife, or another object.

Decoupage. With this fun decorative method, you affix paper designs with matte medium to lamps or other furnishings and seal over the top with the same matte medium.

Dry brushing. Using very little paint on the brush can help achieve many textures. The amount of paint on the brush and the method with which it's applied can create a rough striped or banded effect or a mottled, aged look.

Frottage (fraw-tahj). This is from the French for rubbing. Frottage involves coating a surface with glaze, then creating a textured effect by pressing a material or tool into the glaze. Newspaper, plastic, butcher paper, and rags are common tools for frottage.

Glazing. This technique takes any form that uses glaze as the main medium. Usually glaze mixed with paint or colorant is applied to a surface, then manipulated with a tool. A rag or paper towel can create a cloudy, soft finish while stippling brushes make a tightly spotted pattern.

Stenciling. Stencils are available in craft stores and online and range in shape, size, and cost. Secure the stencil where you'd like it with painter's tape or stencil spray adhesive. Using a stippling brush, with a scant amount of paint on the tips of the bristles, pounce, or tap, the stencil, allowing the paint to leave the brush and press onto the stencil and surface. Remove the stencil to reveal the pattern or design you want. Too much paint bleeds underneath the stencil and creates a blurred line, so blot the brush if necessary to remove excess paint before you pounce. If you can't find a stencil you like, create your own design by cutting it out of posterboard for a unique pattern that's inexpensive and easy to duplicate.

One last note: During any painting project, there are certain materials that are handy to have around at all times. Always be sure to have plenty of rags and sponges for cleaning up messes. Also inlude plastic containers, stir sticks, and paint can visors to the list for just about every project in this book.

ESTIMATING QUANTITY

The quantities for paint, glaze, varnish, and matte medium listed with projects in the book were used in "Fresh Coat" shows and are intended only as guidelines. To estimate paint quantities for your room, measure the perimeter. Multiply the result by the ceiling height to get the total square feet or meters you need to paint. Don't worry about deducting the space taken up by windows and doors unless they add up to more than 100 square feet. Divide the total square feet or meters into the number of square feet or meters that your paint can says it will cover. Round up to the nearest whole number to determine how many cans you'll need.

1

Bedrooms

A bedroom is particularly important because it's our private space. This environment can determine how well we sleep at night and how positive we feel each morning. Treat yourself and your family to bedrooms that are uncluttered and comfortable. No matter what design style or color palette you choose, the bedroom should provide a sense of relaxation and reassurance. Restful, easy colors and fresh, clean furnishings will ease your mind and brighten your day — every day!

Shannon

MOROCCAN BEDROOM

This listless bedroom, with plain white walls and a plain white loft, needs color, flair, and fashion. To liven up the lifeless space, the homeowner turns the room into a Moroccan-style treat, with a sunny backdrop and dramatic shapes to catch the eye.

PROJECT SUMMARY

The first step is to rejuvenate the walls with a golden mix of paint and glaze, enhanced by a glaze on the ceiling to give the appearance of sun-faded tent fabric. Stencils on the walls add a fun touch. Painting the panels in the loft with a lavender star design and adding random sparkles on display shelves add an air of whimsy.

BEFORE: The bedroom has good natural light, but the furnishings were boring (above and below).

AFTER: Blandness is gone as the purple stencils add a fun flair to the walls (right), and the dressers get a desert-like color to complement the painted walls (left).

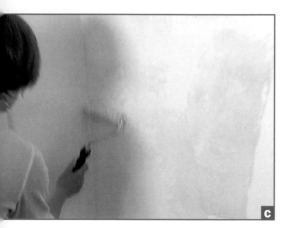

◀ PAINTING THE WALLS ▶

To add to the warm yellow hue of the walls, glaze the ceiling with vertical strokes to play up the sun-washed look. When mixed with paint, the glaze gives a soft, desert feel and makes the paint translucent. Use coarse rosin paper to protect the floor; it gives better traction than loose tarps.

You Will Need

Rosin paper	6" thin rollers
1½" medium-tack painter's tape	Medium trays
1 quart pale orange eggshell finish paint	Paper towels
1 gallon clear glaze	

1 Lay down the rosin paper, and tape it down. Tape off the door, window trim, and baseboards. Mix one part paint to three parts glaze (photo A). Roll on the clear glaze first in sections (photo B).

2 Roll on the glaze mixture in a random pattern to cover about 75 percent of the wall (photo C).

3 Spread the glaze on the wall with a paper towel bunched up into a pad (photo D). Let it dry.

DECORATING THE WALLS WITH STENCILS

The purple stencil was inspired by the room's chandelier, and the color ties in with the lavender curtains and bedding. For more drama, the stencils are applied randomly to draw the eye around the room to shapes and textures.

You Will Need

- Stencil (homemade or from a crafts store)
- 1½" medium-tack painter's tape
- Stippling brushes
- 4 ounces purple paint
- Paper towels
- Plastic containers

1 With the painter's tape, secure the stencil. Dip the stencil brush lightly into the paint to get a small amount on the brush (photo A).

2 Blot excess paint on the paper towel (photo B).

3 Lightly stipple the purple paint on the stencil by dabbing the brush on the stencil (photo C). Remove the stencils, and apply the pattern randomly around the room. Let it dry.

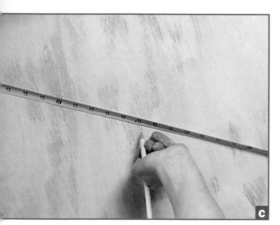

◣ LIGHTENING UP THE LOFT ◢

A simple whitewash gives the loft a more finished look while keeping the design rustic. Add lavender and green decorations in a traditional Moroccan pattern to the panels in the loft to create a colorful tile-inspired effect.

You Will Need

Large plastic container	3" square brushes
Stir sticks	Pencil
1 quart cream paint	Measuring tape
1 quart apple green paint	Posterboard
1 quart lavender paint	Scissors
Water	½" angled artist's brushes

1 Thin the paint with water until the consistency is like a light cream (photo A). Brush the paint onto the woodwork (photo B). Paint the edges of the wood panels beneath the loft with the green paint, thinned if desired.

2 To find the center of each wood panel, stretch the measuring tape from corner to corner, and draw a 2-inch pencil line in the center. Repeat stretching the tape measure between the opposite corners, drawing the 2-inch line at the halfway point; the X will mark the center of the panel. (photo C).

3 Cut out squares from the posterboard; then cut a hole in the center of the posterboard. Find the center X through the cut hole, and trace around the square. Turn the posterboard 90 degrees, and trace around the square again (photo D).

4 With the artist's brush, paint along the outer pencil lines with the lavender paint to make the stars (photo E).

TIPS | DIY Network
Home Improvement

KEEP IT CLEAN

Remember to always paint on a clean surface so the paint will adhere better.

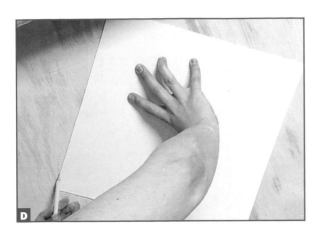

◀ DOLLING UP THE DRESSERS ▶

To give the dressers an exotic look, paint the pieces a deep mustard color using special rollers with a soft nap that won't leave brush marks. Add details using stamps with colors and patterns resembling Moroccan tiles. The stamps nicely enhance the bright drawer pulls, but be careful not to use too much paint on the stamps.

You Will Need

Paint preparation wipes	4 ounces apple green paint
Cardboard	4 ounces red eggshell finish paint
1 quart mustard semi-gloss paint	4 ounces purple paint
2" square brushes	Foam stamps
6" flocked rollers	½" angled artist's brushes
Medium plastic trays	Artist's brushes

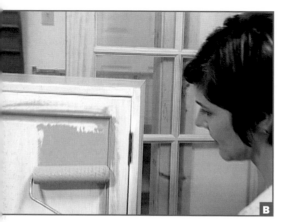

1 Clean the furniture with the wipes. Put cardboard beneath the dresser so you can paint to the bottom (photo A).

2 Cut in by painting the edges, corners, and details with the square brush. Then roll on the rest of the mustard-colored paint on the flat surfaces with the flocked rollers (photo B).

3 With the artist's brush, paint the stamp details in the color you choose (photo C). Then press the stamp on the dresser's surface to transfer the paint (photo D).

◀ **MAKING THE SHELVES SPARKLE** ▶

The shelves are the stars of the room once painted red! Use glitter paint to apply a sparkly gold touch inside, which looks cloudy when it's applied but sparkles when it's dry.

You Will Need

1 quart red eggshell finish paint	Small plastic tray
4 ounces pale orange eggshell finish	Roller with star design
1½" square brushes	1 quart clear glitter paint
1 quart pale gold metallic paint	

1 With the square brushes, apply the red paint to the shelves (photo A). Let it dry. Over the red paint, add the shimmering gold paint to the interior and the shelves with the square brush (photo B).

2 Roll on the star design. Then apply a coat of the clear glitter paint with the square brush (photo C). Let it dry. For more glitter, apply a second coat.

A

B

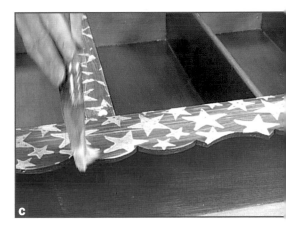
C

WORLDLY BOYS' ROOM

The task here is to create a fun bedroom for two young, adventurous boys. They need an inspiring but calming place to read, relax, and rest. The kids won't believe their eyes when they see the transformation of their room from white and uninviting to colorful and worldly with stars on the ceiling and a map to track their travels.

BEFORE: If the kids yawn in here, it's probably from the boring furnishings, not sleepiness.

◤ PROJECT SUMMARY ◢

The room reaches out to these boys who love to explore with books, maps, and their own excursions. The walls get a soothing new coat to complement a snazzy ceiling filled with a galaxy of star stencils. Plain white shelves are jazzed up with an old-world leather look and some rejuvenated baskets for belongings. And a map of the world, to adorn a wall, lets the boys map their adventures.

AFTER: The boys will reach for the stars under the ceiling's stenciled constellations and dream about their travels with the aged map (above). Fun colors on the baskets make organizing toys a pleasure (left).

A

B

C

PAINTING THE WALLS

A new coat of olive green — not too dark and not too loud — gives a soothing feel to the room and complements the furnishings. You won't need a ladder if you use the roller extender to reach the higher spots.

You Will Need

Screwdrivers	Roller extenders
Rosin paper	Large rollers
1½" medium-tack painter's tape	Trays
2½" angle brushes	2 gallons olive green matte paint
Paint mugs	

1 Tape down the rosin paper to protect the floor (photo A). Remove the light and switch plates.

2 Tape off the window and door moldings (photo B). Tape off the ceiling and floor so the baseboard and ceiling trim gets painted the same as the walls.

3 With the angle brushes, paint the baseboards and ceiling trim. Then cut in with the brushes on the edges (photo C) and corners of the walls (photo D)

TIPS | DIY Network Home Improvement

ROLLING MADE EASY

For easier rolling and to spread the paint more evenly, use a slight "v" pattern when you apply the paint, then roll over the cut-in lines for a smooth finish. Coat the roller regularly, and use the tray to remove excess paint.

4 Roll on the paint with the roller extenders (photo E). Let it dry, repeat if necessary, and remove the tape.

TIPS | DIY Network
Home Improvement

■ **ROLLER COVER**

Wash roller covers in mild soapy water before use. This helps to keep stray fibers from ruining your new paint job

■ **TIME SAVER**

Between coats, place rollers or brushes in self-closing plastic bags and store them in the refrigerator for up to two days. Bring to room temperature before use.

GLAZING AND STENCILING THE CEILING

What child wouldn't love finding their favorite constellations and sleeping under the stars every night? Apply a swirled coat of blue glaze and paint a stenciled galaxy to create a cosmic feel. The last touch is a rocket stencil to launch the kids' dreams.

You Will Need

1½" medium-tack painter's tape	Oversize stippling brushes
6" rollers	Tracing paper with constellations
Trays	4 ounces yellow tempera paint
1 quart dark blue paint	Sample size bright yellow paint
2 quarts clear glaze	Medium and small star stencils
Paint visor	Rocket stencil
Plastic container	Stenciling brushes
Plastic spatula	Paper towels
3" square brushes	Small plastic containers

1 Tape off the ceiling trim. Mix three parts clear glaze to one part of the dark blue paint (photo A).

2 While still wet, roll on the clear glaze over a 2-foot patch of the ceiling (photo B). Then roll on the blue glaze mixture over about 70 percent of the area covered by the clear glaze (photo C).

3 With the square brushes, scrub the blue glaze into the ceiling, creating a swirled, cloudy effect. (photo D). Let it dry.

4 Tape over any stencils not needed for the project (photo E). Dip the stippling brush lightly in the tempera paint, and dab off the extra paint on the paper towels (photo F).

5 Place the medium stencils where you choose on the ceiling, and push on the paint with the stippling brushes (photo G). With the small stencils, stipple on the lighter yellow paint in random patterns (photo H). Stipple on the rocket stencil (photo I).

G

E

H

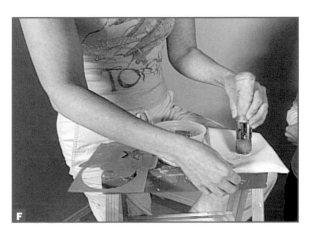

F

I

◢ PAINTING THE SHELVES AND BASKETS ◣

After you brush on the oil primer made for slick surfaces, the boring, white shelves get a classy, leathery look. Paint in a criss-crossing motion, and then roll a rag through the glaze to create a rugged feel. A map-inspired color scheme brightens up the baskets and provides a fun way to organize toys.

You Will Need

150-grit sandpaper	Clean rags
Face mask	2" square brushes
Tack cloths	2" angle brushes
1½" medium-tack painter's tape	4" rollers
2" foam brushes	Sample size pale yellow paint
1 quart specialty bonding primer tinted to medium brown paint	Sample size pale green paint
1 quart clear glaze	Sample size pale orange paint
1 quart reddish brown paint	Sample size pale blue paint
Sample size dark brown paint	1 quart varnish
Plastic containers	

1 Wearing the face masks, sand the furniture. Use the tack cloths to remove the dust and grit. Remove the shelves and baskets. Tape off the tops of the furniture (photo A).

2 Apply the tinted primer with the foam brushes (photo B), and let it dry. With the square brushes, using very little paint, use a crisscross motion to apply the reddish brown paint (photo C). Make sure to let the under coat show through. Let it dry.

3 Mix one part glaze to three parts of the dark brown paint. Roll on a light coat of the brown glaze with the 4" rollers .

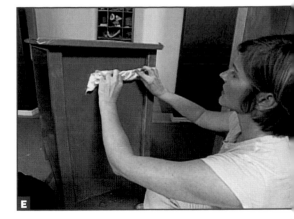

4 Twist the clean rags (photo D), then roll the rags through the glaze (photo E). Let it dry.

5 Apply the varnish with the 2" square brushes (photo F). Let it dry. Remove the tape.

6 With the pale paints and angle brushes, paint the baskets on the inside and outside (photo G). Let them dry. Replace the shelves and baskets.

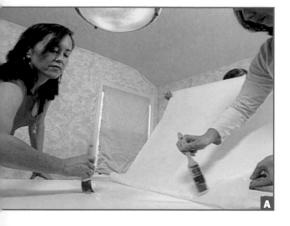

◀ MAKING THE WALL MAP ▶

Create a great way for the kids to remember their travels with this map, which they can decorate with pins to indicate where they've been. Tea stains give an aged look to the map, an appearance you can enhance by spattering brown paint on top.

You Will Need

World map	16 ounces matte medium
Foam core board	1½" square brushes
Utility knife	Toothbrushes
Straightedge	Tea bags
Measuring tape	Sample size dark brown paint
Plastic spreader	
Surface to cut the foam core board on	

1 Brew the tea bags in water, and let them cool. Cut the foam core board to size.

2 With the square brush, apply the matte medium to the foam core board and to the back of the map (photo A).

3 Use the spreader to press out the wrinkles and air bubbles in the map as you attach it to the foam core board (photo B). Repeat the process a small section at a time. Apply a final coat of matte medium to the front of the map, and let it dry.

4 With the square brush, apply a light coat of tea to the map (photo C).

5 Dip the toothbrushes in the brown paint (photo D), and flick the brushes at the map to spatter the paint (photo E). Let it dry.

DIY Network
Home Improvement

STICKY BUSINESS

Matte medium is available in art stores, while decoupage kits can be found in most craft stores.

CITY SUITE

It's time to give this boring studio apartment some fresh air. The solution is to turn it into a classy city suite with color and pattern. The owner of the small, cluttered condo wants a more expansive space, and that's accomplished by creating two distinct areas for sleeping and dining.

PROJECT SUMMARY

Start with the bedroom area, which is enhanced with a coat of soft lavender paint for a soothing space to watch city life. A playful floral pattern on the closet door enriches the inviting mood. Stick-on stencils give the drama of wallpaper without the work. The vanity gets a face-lift with different treatments for the top and bottom to add drama. Lastly, the nightstands shine with a fresh wash of paint.

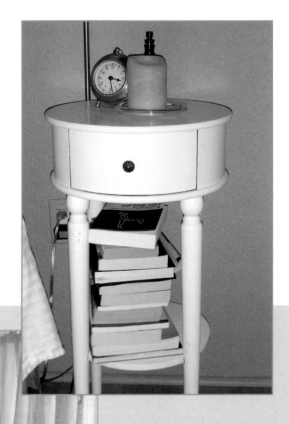

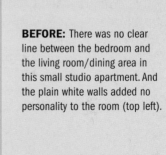

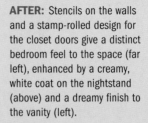

BEFORE: There was no clear line between the bedroom and the living room/dining area in this small studio apartment. And the plain white walls added no personality to the room (top left).

AFTER: Stencils on the walls and a stamp-rolled design for the closet doors give a distinct bedroom feel to the space (far left), enhanced by a creamy, white coat on the nightstand (above) and a dreamy finish to the vanity (left).

◢ PAINTING THE WALLS AND CEILING AND STENCILING ◣

Use an extension roller to paint the ceiling, and keep it loaded with paint to give good coverage on the textured surface. For stenciling, burnishing—or smoothing out surfaces—is especially important on textured walls because it helps you get the stencil into crevices.

You Will Need

- Rosin paper
- 1½" medium-tack painter's tape
- Dust brushes
- Screwdrivers
- 3 gallons lavender matte finish paint
- Paint mugs
- 2" angle brushes
- Large rollers
- Large trays
- Roller extenders
- Adhesive stencils
- Plastic spreader (available at paint or home improvement stores)
- 6" rollers
- Small trays
- 1 gallon dark lilac matte finish paint
- Craft knife
- Stippling brushes
- Paper towels

1 Tape down the rosin paper, and remove all the plates for switches and outlets. With the angle brush, cut in by painting the edges and corners with the lavender matte finish paint (photo A). Let it dry, and repeat if needed. With the roller extender, paint the ceiling and walls with the lavender matte (photo B).

2 With the self-adhesive stencils, create a pattern on the focal wall of the dining room (photo C). A wide, staggered pattern will give a wallpaper effect.

3 Peel off the stencil backing (photo D), and push the stencil against the wall. Use the plastic spreader to make the stencil stick flat (photo E).

TIPS | DIY Network
Home Improvement

TAPING ROSIN PAPER

Rosin paper is a heavy red or brown paper often used by contractors to protect new floors during building. It works great on hard floors, but be sure to tape it down to prevent slipping.

4 Put a little of the dark lilac matte finish paint on the edge of the stippling brush, and wipe off the excess with the paper towels (photo F).

5 With the stippling brush, tap on the stencils with paint (photo G). Then with the angle brush, cut in with the dark lilac paint. Use the 6 inch rollers to apply the paint around the stencils (photo H), then coat the rest of the wall with the regular rollers. Let it dry, and apply another coat if needed. Use the craft knife to pull off the stencil smoothly (photo I).

STAMP-ROLLING THE CLOSET

Prepare the doors by rubbing on trisodium phosphate to remove the old sheen and help the new paint stick. The base coat is the same color as the paint on the walls, but for the closet, a pearl finish is used because it's more durable. Then use a stamp-rolling technique, which applies a pattern that's on the rubber roller.

You Will Need

Trisodium phosphate	6" flocked roller
Rubber gloves	Level
Bucket of warm water	Pencil
Sponges	Straightedge
1½" medium-tack painter's tape	Specialty stamp roller
Dropcloth	Rubber roller
2 quarts lavender in pearl finish paint	Double roller
1 quart white in pearl finish paint	Foam roller
Small tray	

1 Wearing the rubber gloves, wash the closet doors with the sponges and trisodium phosphate (photo A).

2 Tape off the closet door edges with the painter's tape (photo B), and put the dropcloth on the floor.

3 For a smooth finish, roll the lavender paint on the closet doors with the flocked rollers, and let it dry (photo C). Use the level, pencil, and straightedge to draw vertical lines for the stamp-roller pattern (photo D, next page).

4 Remove the rubber roller from the double roller, and dip the foam roller in the white paint (photo E, next page).

5 Reattach the rubber roller (photo F), and roll the pattern against the foam roller to prepare to paint.

6 Roll the pattern on the closet doors (photo G), and let it dry.

D

F

E

G

PAINTING THE VANITY

With plain kitchen sponges, this dark, uninspiring desk was transformed into a fresh, dreamy vanity. The fine-nap rollers used are made for wood to give a smooth finish without brush marks. By adding a few drops of concentrated color to the textured paint and sponging on the paint, the desktop gets the shimmering effect of stone.

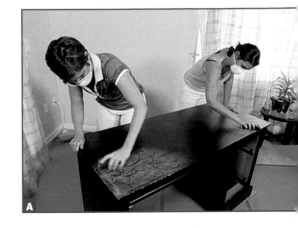

A

You Will Need

Screwdrivers	1 quart light green satin finish paint
Face mask	Sponges
Sandpaper	2-ounce tube of taupe tint
Dust brush	3 small trays
Tack cloth	3 small plastic containers
2" square brushes	Stir sticks
1½ inch medium-tack painter's tape	Wide putty knives
1 quart primer tinted 50 percent to light green	Spatula
6" flocked rollers	Cardboard
2-ounce tube of dark brown tint	1 quart flat varnish
2 quarts Shimmer Stone	

B

1 With the screwdriver, take off the drawer pulls and, wearing the face mask, sand the piece (photo A). Use the dust brush to remove the residue; then wipe the desk clean with the tack cloth (photo B).

2 Cut in on the edges and corners with the square brush. Using the flocked rollers, roll on the primer, and let it dry.

3 Use the painter's tape to tape off the top of the desk. Repeat the above step with the light green paint (photo C). Let it dry and remove the tape.

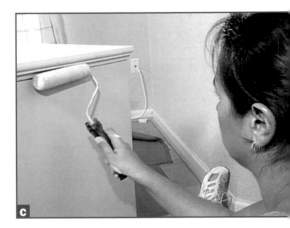

C

4 Mix the dark brown tint into one quart of the Shimmer Stone (photo D) Add a little at a time to get the right mix. With the sponges, put a solid coat on the top (photo E). Let it dry.

5 Pounce, or dab, lightly with the sponge to get a stone texture (photo F). Then mix the taupe tint with one quart of the Shimmer Stone. With the sponges, put a solid coat on top, and let it dry.

6 With the square brushes, apply the varnish to the top surface (photo G). Reattach the drawer pulls.

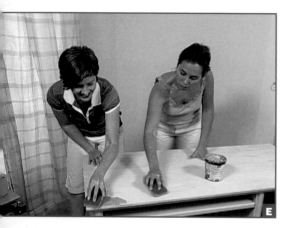

PAINTING THE NIGHTSTANDS

Freshen up these peices with a coat of creamy white paint. The nightstands have a shiny top coat, so they are sanded thoroughly to make the paint stick. Use sandpaper with foam on the back, which makes it easier to work around the furniture details. This final project helps lighten up the room and makes it more cheerful.

You Will Need

Screwdrivers	Tack cloth
Dropcloths	1 quart white pearl finish paint
Cardboard	1 quart primer tinted 50 percent to light green
1½" medium-tack painter's tape	2" square brushes
Face masks	
Foam sanding blocks	

1 Remove the drawer pulls. Wearing the face mask, sand the pieces (photo A). Then use the tack cloth to wipe off the residue (photo B).

2 Put the cardboard beneath the furniture so you can paint the pieces to the bottom. Use the square brushes to paint the nightstands with the tinted primer (photo C). Let the primer dry.

3 Use the square brushes to paint the nightstands with the white pearl finish paint (photo D). Let the paint dry.

2

Living Rooms

For many of us, living rooms have changed from formal spaces to any room in the house where we can hang out with friends and family. For some people, it's the basement, dining room, or even a section of the garage, any place where people can chill out. Comfort is key here, so easy traffic patterns and comfortable colors work wonders. The living room should feel expansive, too. Consider subtle wall colors that look great with artwork, earthy tones that make furnishings feel relaxed, and bold accent colors where your personal style shines through.

Shannon

CLUB LOUNGE

This cluttered dining room with yard-sale furniture doesn't honor the Victorian home it's in. Some urban class will rescue the room—think dramatic color contrasts, a cool contemporary design on furniture, and the look of Italian tiles on a table.

BEFORE: Built-in bookshelves and wainscoting lend character to the room, but it needs a splash of color to make the architectural details pop.

◣ PROJECT SUMMARY ◥

The homeowner wants to turn the formal dining room into a chic lounge perfect for entertaining with music and food. The traditional architectural details are attractive, but the paint scheme has to go. A new dark and light color contrast on the walls and ceiling add drama, and a two-layer, tile-pattern stencil turn a plain table into an exotic Italian piece. Marble cubes are transformed into stylish furniture with some modern designs, and a vibrant fabric covered with special phrases adorn another table.

AFTER: The chic, new wall color provides a nice contrast for the bright white trim and decorative painting techniques used on the room's various pieces of furniture give them a custom high-end look.

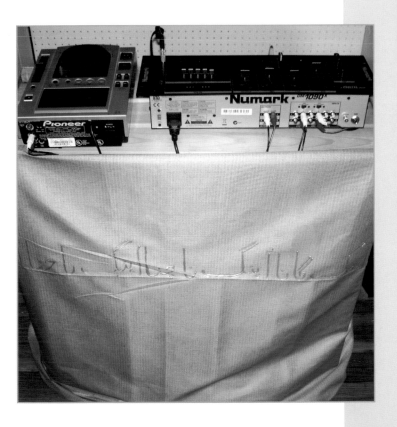

PAINTING THE WALLS AND CEILING

Paint the ceiling beams white to match other architectural details in the room and add a sense of height and drama. The walls get a rich brown coat for a vibrant contrast. Use fine-napped rollers on the trim for a smooth surface.

You Will Need

Rosin paper	2 quarts of white eggshell finish paint
1½" medium-tack painter's tape	1 gallon dark brown matte finish paint
Face mask	
Tack cloths	2 quarts of white primer
150-grit sandpaper or sanding blocks	Large trays
2" angle brushes	4" rollers
Large rollers	

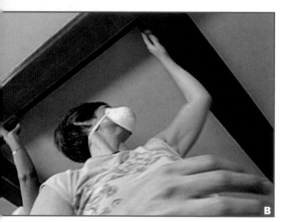

1 Roll out the rosin paper in strips, and tape it to the floor (photo A).

2 Wearing the face mask, sand the ceiling beams (photo B), and wipe away the dust with the tack cloths (photo C).

3 With the angle brushes, cut in with the primer on the trim and ceiling beams (photo D), and let it dry. Then use the 4" rollers to apply the primer to the flat surfaces, and let it dry.

4 With the angle brushes, cut in with the white paint on the trim and beams, let it dry, and repeat if needed. Use the 4" rollers to apply the paint (photo E).

5 With the brush, cut in with the brown paint on the walls, and then use the large rollers to apply the paint (photo F). Let it dry, and repeat if needed.

TIPS | DIY Network
Home Improvement

PAINTING TRIM

Professionals paint trim first, using tape to protect the walls, if needed. Trim should always be sanded and all needed repairs should be made before painting; this helps create a clean, professional look.

DECORATING THE CONTACT PAPERED CUBES

These throw-away pieces are transformed into chic seats (or tables) with a modern design from some stretchy painting tape and a cheery coat of yellow paint. A special primer is used that prepares such surfaces, making new painting a breeze.

You Will Need

1 quart specialty bonding primer	Specialty flexible painting tape
2" foam brushes	1 quart clear varnish
Small trays	1 quart yellow matte finish paint
4" rollers	Artist's brushes
1 quart white matte finish paint	

1 Elevate the pieces from the floor so you can paint to the bottom (photo A).

2 With the foam brushes, apply the primer (photo B). Let it dry.

3 Use the rollers to apply the white base coat (photo C). Let it dry.

4 Use the flexible painting tape to make wavy stripes all around the sides of the cube (photo D).

TIPS | DIY Network
Home Improvement

REMOVING TAPE

Make sure the paint dries well before you remove the tape so the paint doesn't peel off as you pull.

5 With the artist's brushes, apply the varnish to the tape edges (photo E).

6 Roll on the yellow paint (photo F), and let it dry. Repeat if it's necessary. Remove the tape (photo G).

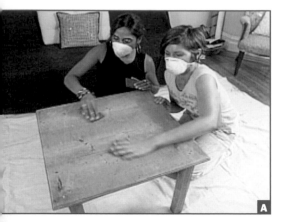

◣ STENCILING THE TABLE ◢

This yard-sale table is given an exotic look with an Italian-influenced tile pattern from a two-layer stencil. First, a base coat of the brown paint is used on the walls to provide a classy background.

You Will Need

Medium-grit foam sanding pads	Paper towels
Face mask	1 quart primer
Tack cloths	Sample size lavender paint
2" foam brushes	Sample size yellow paint
Spatula	1 quart dark brown paint
Stencils	Sample size tan paint
6 stippling brushes	

1 Wearing the face mask, use the foam sanders to sand the table (photo A), and remove the dust with the tack cloths.

2 Mix the brown paint with the primer. Use the foam brushes to apply the primer (photo B), and let it dry.

3 With the foam brushes, apply a base coat of the brown paint (photo C), and let it dry.

4 Dip the tip of the stippling brush in the paint (photo D), and dab off the excess on the paper towels (photo E).

5 Hold the stencil in place on the tabletop, and stipple the brush on the stencil by pushing the brush up and down, not rubbing (photo F). Stipple in the lavender and tan paints. Let it dry.

E

F

6 Stipple on the second stencil layer in yellow (photo G). Then use the foam brush to apply the varnish (photo H). Let it dry.

◢ PAINTING FABRIC FOR THE SHELF ◣

This lively fabric brightens up the piece of furniture and shows off the homeowner's creativity. The cloth is decorated with words from her native language written in fabric paint, a washable medium. Artist's brushes, which have fine points and are good for detail work, help complete the job.

You Will Need

Fabric of your choosing	Small, pointed artist's brushes
Pencil	Paper dropcloth
Fabric paints	Thumbtacks

1 Lay the fabric out flat. Draw your designs on the fabric in pencil first (photo A).

2 Using the fabric paints and artist's brushes, paint over the pencil (photo B). Let it dry.

3 If needed, apply a second layer of fabric paint to highlight your work (photo C). With the thumbtacks, attach the fabric to the front and sides of the shelf.

TIPS | DIY Network Home Improvement

MIXING IT UP

Adding a bit of paint to primer can help create good coverage with color. Keep the mixture to less than 50 percent paint so the primer will keep its strength.

diy network

FAMILY PLAYROOM

This room screams for color and life to turn an uninviting space into a fun, family-friendly place. A comprehensive touch transforms everything, from the dull tones of the furniture and the dated vertical blinds to the uninspiring fireplace that offers lots of potential.

◢ **PROJECT SUMMARY** ◣

A warm, smoky, plum color on the walls provides a neutral complement for the new raspberry and green hues that brighten the furniture in the room. For the cinder block fireplace, filling in the mortar lines between the bricks and putting plaster over the top adds texture and gives the room a rustic feel. The blinds receive a darker shade of the wall color to tie things together.

BEFORE: This home's expansive downstairs was being underutilized and over the years had become a catch all for various odds and ends, including uninspired furniture (above and right).

AFTER: With its new faux-stone finish, the fireplace is now the focal point of this family-friendly space (left). Warm tones on the vertical blinds are enhanced by a welcoming, homey color on the walls (right), while red painted chairs add a splash of color to the room (above).

◢ PAINTING THE WALLS ◣

Warm up a room by coating the walls with a cozy color. Start with a tinted primer for the base coat, then roll on a juicy plum shade.

You Will Need

Dropcloths	2 gallons muted plum eggshell finish paint
1½" medium-tack painter's tape	2" angle brushes
Dust brushes	Large rollers
Screwdrivers	Large trays
2 gallons primer tinted 50 percent to muted plum	Roller extenders
1 quart dark taupe eggshell finish paint	

1 Put dropcloths on the floor, and tape down the edges of the cloths (photo A). Remove all the plates for switches and outlets.

2 To apply the tinted primer, cut in on the edges and corners with the angle brushes, then use the roller extenders to roll the walls with the primer (photo B). Let it dry.

3 Repeat step two using the muted plum paint. Let dry and repeat if needed.

REVIVING THE BLINDS

Vertical blinds can be a total eyesore. To remedy this, spray on a primer designed for slick surfaces. Apply two tones of paint, mostly using the wall's color, but a few blinds get a darker shade to suggest a subtle pattern.

You Will Need

Screwdrivers	1 quart taupe eggshell finish paint
Face mask	1 quart light reddish brown eggshell finish paint
Dropcloth	
3 spray cans specialty bonding primer	Small trays
	4" rollers
Spray nozzles	

A

B

1 With the screwdrivers, remove the blinds from the walls, and lay them flat.

2 Wearing the face mask, spray the entire surface with the clear primer (photo A). Let the primer dry.

3 Roll on the taupe eggshell paint (photo B), and then roll on the light reddish brown eggshell to create a striped effect. Let the paint dry.

A

B

C

◣ WARMING UP THE COFFEE TABLE ◢

After spraying the primer, add stripes of color and a fun pattern on top. Once the stripes are taped off, the edge of the tape line is sealed with a little varnish so the paint won't bleed underneath the line. A good coat of varnish protects the surface and the artwork.

You Will Need

Cardboard	Blow-dryer
Dropcloths	1 quart varnish in satin finish
Face mask	Sample size cornflower blue paint
1 spray can specialty bonding primer	Sample size light blue paint
Spray nozzles	Sample size light green
Tinted primer	Sample size grass green
6" flocked rollers	Sample size dark gray paint
Tape measure	1 quart primer tinted to light green
Pencil	Small plastic squeeze bottle
T square	

1 Put dropcloths down, and place cardboard under the table so you can paint it to the bottom. Wearing a face mask, spray on the clear primer (photo A), and let it dry.

2 Roll on the tinted primer (photo B), and let it dry.

3 With the T square, tape measure, and pencil, mark off four stripes. Then tape off two stripes for painting (photo C).

4 Seal the tape edge with a little varnish (photo D). Then roll on two stripes in two colors (photo E), let it dry, and apply another coat. Let it dry again.

5 Tape off the other two stripes, seal the tape with varnish, and roll on the other two colors. Let it dry, and apply a second coat.

6 Pour the dark gray paint into the squeeze bottle, and squeeze the paint onto the center of the table in a circular motion in any pattern you want (photo F). Let it dry. Then roll on the varnish (photo G).

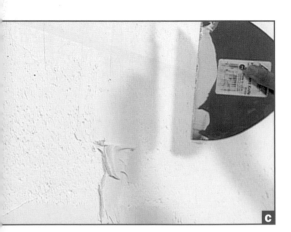

◢ UPGRADING THE FIREPLACE ◣

The cinder block fireplace gets a makeover with plaster and wax for a rustic stone look. The pre-tinted specialty plaster is more expensive, but it stays wet longer than standard plaster and allows for more time to work the surface. Acrylic wax is used to bring out variations in the plaster.

You Will Need

1½" medium-tack painter's tape	1 quart primer tinted 50 percent to taupe
Ceramic tile adhesive	4" rollers
Mud pans	Small trays
Plastic trowels	Large plastic container
Hawks	Spatula
Medium putty knives	2 gallons Marmarino plaster
Large sponges	1 gallon acrylic wax
Large plastic container with water	5-6 drops universal tint in raw umber

1 Tape the edges of the fireplace (photo A). Scoop the ceramic tile adhesive into the mud pans (photo B).

2 With the medium putty knives, fill in the mortar lines with the adhesive (photo C), and feather out the edges to blend it into the surface. Before the surface dries, use the damp sponges to smooth the surface (photo D). Let it dry.

3 Scoop the plaster onto the hawk, and then scoop it onto the trowel (photo E). Trowel on a thin coat of the plaster to cover the entire surface (photo F).

4 As the plaster begins to set, burnish it by smoothing out the plaster with the flat side of the trowel (photo G). Let it dry.

5 Mix the universal tint in raw umber into the acrylic wax, and trowel on a thin coat (photo H). Let it dry. Burnish it with the trowel again to soften the sheen.

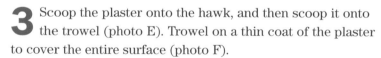

TIPS | DIY Network
Home Improvement

MIXING IT UP
Acrylic wax is clear, so it can be mixed with colorant for a thin layer of color.

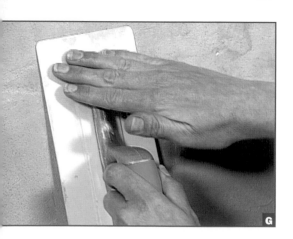

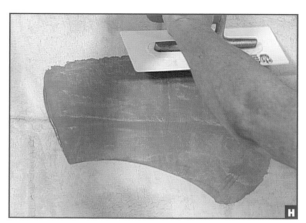

CHEERING UP THE CHAIRS

A fun raspberry shade adds a dash of color and livens up this area of the room. First, sand the wood to help the paint stick, then apply primer and paint.

You Will Need

- Screwdrivers
- Dropcloths
- Face mask
- Sandpaper
- Tack cloth

- 1 quart primer tinted 50 percent to hot pink
- 1 quart raspberry pearl finish paint
- Small foam brushes

1 With the screwdrivers, remove the seats from the chair if possible and sand the chairs (photo A). With the tack cloth, wipe the dust from the chairs (photo B).

2 With the foam brush, apply the tinted primer, and let it dry (photo C). Then apply a coat of the raspberry paint. Let dry and repeat if needed

diy
network

COLLECTOR'S LIVING ROOM

This dull, drab room is a victim of lusterless color — too much beige. To make the space feel bigger and more inviting, the room needs a warmer feel and a way to enhance the furniture. That calls for a mix of texture, color, and pattern.

◀ **PROJECT SUMMARY** ▶

The solution to the blandness is to rescue the room with dramatic colors, three-dimensional art, and a fish-scale design. To start, freshen the walls with a deep color. An art project with painted tiles creates a needed focal point in the room. The furniture and furnishings also get face-lifts. Added texture to the cupboard and painted stripes on the curtains make the living room much more livable.

BEFORE: This living room was tastefully decorated with the homeowner's favorite collections, but it lacked color and focus.

AFTER: A striped pattern on the newly painted curtains extends the room's hip design theme to the windows.

AFTER: Dramatic paint on the walls and ceilings showcase the homeowner's furniture and the one-of-a-kind artwork blends well with his existing collections.

A

B

C

PAINTING THE WALLS AND CEILING

A rich tobacco color on the walls makes the room feel warmer and creates a more visible presence for the furniture. Painting the ceiling an eggplant color using a crisscross pattern allows some of the original color to show through to add depth and texture. A metallic glaze on the ceiling gives a luxurious, three-dimensional sense.

You Will Need

Rosin paper	1 gallon tobacco brown matte
1½" medium-tack painter's tape	2½" square brushes
½"-1" artist's brushes	Large plastic containers
1 quart varnish	6 sponges
2" angle brushes	1 quart dark violet matte
Large rollers	4 ounces bronze metallic paint
Paint trays	4 ounces gold metallic paint
Paint mugs	1 quart clear glaze
Paint can visor	

1 Tape down the rosin paper to protect the floor, and tape the trim. With the artist's brush, seal the tape with the varnish. Let it dry.

2 For the walls, use the angle brush to cut in with the brown matte (photo A). Paint the edges and corners with the brown matte. Use the rollers to paint the rest of the walls. Apply a second coat if needed. Let the paint dry completely.

3 Seal the tape around the ceiling trim with varnish. With the square brushes, paint the ceiling in a crisscross pattern with the dark violet matte (photo B), and be sure to allow some of the original color to show through (photo C).

4 Mix the bronze and gold paints with clear glaze to a metallic tone you like. With a new household sponge, scrub the glaze into the ceiling surface. Rub the glaze evenly in small circles to create a pattern (photo D). Then remove the tape from the molding.

TIPS | DIY Network
Home Improvement

GLAZE

Glaze is a clear medium that makes paint and other colorants translucent.

CREATING THE ARTWORK

To create this project, paint cardboard tiles a dark green and mount the tiles above the sofa. Use the dry-brushing technique that involves just a little paint so the cardboard isn't overloaded. Gold paint along the tops of the tiles adds a three-dimensional quality.

You Will Need

12-18 three-dimensional, sculptural cardboard wall tiles	4 ounces forest green paint
1"-2" artist's brushes	Double-stick adhesive
4 ounces gold mica paint	

1 Before you start putting tiles on the wall, figure out the layout on the floor (photo A).

2 Paint the tiles by dry-brushing them with the green paint (photo B).

3 With the artist's brush, add the gold paint to the tops of the tiles (photo C). Let the tiles dry completely.

4 Put up the wall tiles with the double-stick adhesive (photo D).

◢ JAZZING UP THE CUPBOARD ▶

Texture, drama, and color transforms this big piece of furniture. A dark green color on the bottom and a lighter sea-foam color on top is enhanced by a fish-scale pattern on the door panels. Apply the fish pattern with masking fluid, which dries clear, then glaze over the medium, and rub it off to reveal the pattern. Stippling brushes add texture, and a metallic acrylic on the trim gives some glamour.

You Will Need

150-grit sandpaper	Large stippling brushes
Dust brush	4 ounces sea-foam green egshell finish paint
Tack cloth	
Painter's tape	1 quart clear glaze
1 quart primer tinted 50 percent to forest green	4" rollers
	Small trays
2" square brushes	Pointed artist's brushes
Pencil	1 quart satin varnish
Ruler	Golden iridescent pearl tint
Masking fluid	

1 Sand the piece so the paint will adhere. Brush off the dust, and wipe away the residue with the tack cloth. Then prop the furniture with cardboard so you can paint the bottom (photo A).

2 Put tape around the doors to get a clean paint line. Brush on the tinted forest green primer in the crisscross pattern you used for the ceiling to create texture and depth. Let it dry completely.

3 Using the ruler and pencil, draw a grid on the door panels to give an outline of where to put the fish pattern. With the masking fluid and artist's brushes, paint the fish-scale design (photo B). Let it dry completely.

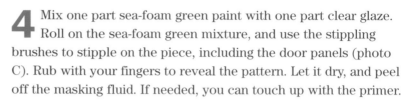

4 Mix one part sea-foam green paint with one part clear glaze. Roll on the sea-foam green mixture, and use the stippling brushes to stipple on the piece, including the door panels (photo C). Rub with your fingers to reveal the pattern. Let it dry, and peel off the masking fluid. If needed, you can touch up with the primer.

5 Brush on the golden iridescent pearl tint around the trim for a finished look (photo D)

6 In a crisscross pattern, apply the varnish, tinted with the forest green paint, to the entire piece. Let it dry. This will protect the piece and give more texture (photo E).

◀ ADDING STRIPES TO THE CURTAINS ▶

Painting pinstripes on the curtains in shades used in the ceiling and on the cupboard adds detail, pulls the colors together, and draws attention to that area of the room. It's best to stick with thin, flat fabrics like cotton or linen because they take paint better than other fabrics.

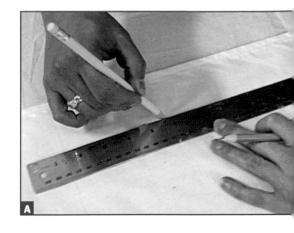

You Will Need	
Pencil	Small plastic container
Straightedge	1-2 sample sizes dark violet paint
8 ounces bronze metallic paint	Medium artist's brushes

1 Lay the fabric out flat. With the pencil and straightedge, measure the stripes to be about 3 inches wide, and draw lines down the fabric (photo A).

2 Paint the bronze stripes over the pencil lines with a medium artist's brush (photo B). Let dry

3 Paint pinstripes in the dark violet color on either side of the bronze stripe

TIPS | DIY Network
Home Improvement

THINK THIN

It's best to stick with thin, flat fabrics like cotton or linen because they take paint better than other fabrics.

Kitchens

Cooking is about motion and energy, and white cabinets and plain walls have taken a back seat to the energetic colors and varied design schemes in modern kitchens. The pages ahead are filled with all the delicious details you need to achieve the look you want. Be inspired by delicate seasonings and beautiful foods. A boring kitchen is like a bland dish, so spice it up with a good recipe of assorted colors, textures, and tastes. Add your own personal touches, and rediscover this space for yourself and your friends.

Shannon

diy network

TRADITIONAL KITCHEN

This bland kitchen with plain cabinets needs spice, flavor, and color to make it a room where the home-owner enjoys cooking for herself and friends. To transform it into a fun place where people can congregate means serving up a makeover. The recipe includes texture and other ingredients that add zest but maintain a classic and elegant touch.

◀ PROJECT SUMMARY ▶

Create a kitchen with rich accents of color. The walls get a warm, soft, golden hue to tie in with hues around the house. A tile pattern for the backsplash becomes the room's focal point with an attractive pattern. A two-tone face-lift for the cabinets draw the eyes, and the café table transports you to Europe with a new finish. A juicy new shade for the ceramic pots connects the color dots.

BEFORE: This kitchen was certainly well-equipped and functional, but it's generic cabinetry and furnishings left the room feeling cold and uninviting.

AFTER: The tiled backsplash and repainted cabinets give the room personality and the bistro-style table gives friends a place to sit and visit while the homeowner cooks.

TIPS | DIY Network Home Improvement

REMOVING TAPE

To avoid the common problem of pulling paint off the wall when removing tape, simply score the edge with a utility knife and pull the tape back at a 45-degree angle.

◢ PAINTING THE WALLS ◣

Matte finish paint is a good choice for the kitchen because it's easily washable without being shiny. A mustard color is selected to warm up this space.

You Will Need

1½" medium-tack painter's tape	2" angle brushes
Dust brushes	Large rollers
Screwdrivers	Large trays
1 gallon mustard yellow matte finish	Roller extenders
Paint mugs	

1 Tape off the countertops and cabinets along the walls and floor (photo A). With the screwdriver, remove all the plates for switches and outlets.

2 Cut in on the edges and corners with the angle brush (photo B).

3 With the rollers and roller extenders, apply the mustard yellow matte finish paint (photo C). Let it dry, and apply a second coat if needed.

A

B

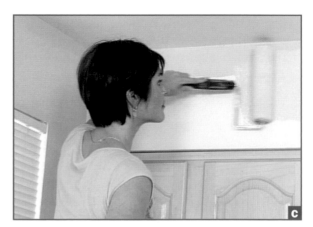

C

◀ TILING THE BACKSPLASH ▶

Tiling is an easy way to add texture and pattern. After cutting in, roll on the base coat with the mini-roller, which is a good size to cover small areas and allows you to work more quickly. To determine the size of tiles to use, measure the backsplash from top to bottom, and divide it in half. Auto-detailing tape, used to pinstripe cars, comes in different widths. Use a narrow size to create a grout line for the tiles.

You Will Need

1 quart cream semi-gloss paint	2" rollers
1 quart dark mustard semi-gloss paint	6" rollers
1 quart sage green semi-gloss	Small trays
1 quart dark gray in matte finish	Blue auto-detailing tape
1½" medium-tack painter's tape	Straightedge
Measuring tape	Level
2" angle brushes	Pencil

1 Put the painter's tape underneath the cabinets and along the counter. Cut in with the angle brush, and use the 6" rollers to roll on the dark gray paint (photo A). Let it dry.

2 Measure the backsplash with the measuring tape, and divide it in half to get the size of the tiles (photo B). To start marking off the pattern with the pencil and the level, draw a horizontal line along the center point (photo C). Start in the center, and work your way out by making pencil marks every 10 inches along the horizontal line.

3 Draw a horizontal pencil line 5 inches above and below the center line. Make 10 inch marks along both lines, staggering them from the center line. Using the auto-detailing tape, connect the dots to create your tile pattern.

4 With the 2" rollers, apply the paint in the various colors (photo D). Let it dry, and roll on a second coat if needed. Remove the tape.

D

RE-CREATING THE CABINETS

The shape of the cabinets is traditional, but the finish is dated. Paint the lower cabinets with an off-black color to anchor the room and break up the blandness. The upper cabinets get a light cream color for a classic look. For a very smooth finish, use rollers with a fine nap.

A

You Will Need

Foam sanding blocks	2 quarts cream pearl finish paint
Face masks	2 quarts off-black pearl finish paint
Dust brush	2" angle brushes
Tack cloths	Small trays
1½" medium-tack painter's tape	6" flocked rollers
2 quarts primer tinted 50 percent to cream paint	Paint mugs
2 quarts primer tinted 50 percent to off-black paint	

B

1 Wearing the face mask, sand the cabinets and casings (photo A). With the dust brush, wipe off the residue, and rub with the tack cloth for a clean surface (photo B).

2 Use the painter's tape to tape the edges of the cabinets for clean lines.

3 Cut in by brushing the cream primer on the upper cabinet doors, and then roll on the primer. Cut in by brushing the off-black primer on the lower cabinet doors, and then roll on the primer (photo C). Let it dry.

4 Cut in by brushing the cream paint on the upper cabinets, and then roll on the paint. Cut in by brushing the off-black paint on the lower cabinets, and then roll on the paint. Let it dry, and apply a second coat if necessary.

C

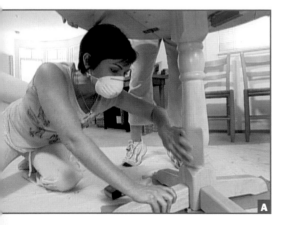

◄ PAINTING THE CAFÉ TABLE ►

Add a taste of Europe to any table by painting the wooden base with a weathered bronze color and topping it off with a limestone look. Use a sea sponge roller and stippling brush to create an elegant finish. A tinted varnish and coat of dark brown paint gives a last layer of texture to the top. Apply a rusting solution to the base for an attractive patina.

You Will Need

Face mask	6 ounces patina solution
Foam sanding blocks	Sample size sage green paint
Sandpaper	1 quartclear glaze
Tack cloth	2 drops universal tint in raw umber
2" square brushes	1 quart flat varnish
1 quart primer tinted 50 percent to dark gray paint	Plastic containers
6 ounces bronze metallic surfacer	Small trays
Sea sponge rollers	Dry brush for blending
1 quart mustard eggshell finish paint	Stencil brushes
1 quart tan eggshell finish paint	Dust brushes
½"-1" artist's brushes	

1 Wearing the face mask, sand the table (photo A), and wipe it clean with the tack cloth (photo B).

2 With the square brushes, paint the pedestal and stem in the dark gray primer (photo C). While the pedestal is drying, paint the table top with the mustard paint (photo D). Let it dry.

3 With the square brush, paint the pedestal with the metallic bronze paint (photo E). Let it dry. Using the sea sponge wrapped around the roller, apply the tan paint to the tabletop (photo F). Let it dry.

D

E

F

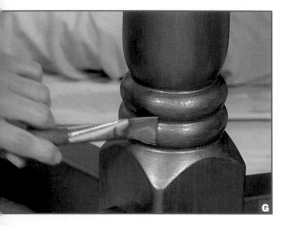

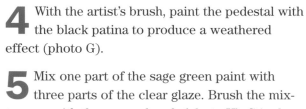

4 With the artist's brush, paint the pedestal with the black patina to produce a weathered effect (photo G).

5 Mix one part of the sage green paint with three parts of the clear glaze. Brush the mixture on with the square brush (photo H). Stipple the paint to blend it and leave a smoother finish (photo I). Let it dry.

6 Add the universal tint to the flat varnish to tint the varnish. With the square brush, apply the varnish, stipple, and blend it using the same technique as with the glaze (photo J).

PAINTING THE POTS

The final dish in this makeover meal is spiffing up the ceramic canisters. Spray painting spicy colors adds some curve to balance the geometric patterns of the new tiles. Emphasize the curve in the canisters by rubbing a little paint across the details to highlight the relief.

You Will Need

1 spray can specialty bonding primer	Household sponge
Face mask	Sample size cream paint
Dropcloths	Chip brushes
1 spray can specialty terra cotta texture paint	

1 Wearing the face mask, spray the pots with the primer (photo A). Let it dry.

2 Wearing the face mask, spray on the terra cotta textured paint (photo B). Let it dry.

3 Use the chip brush to spread a little of the cream paint on the sponge. Then gently rub the sponge on the pots.

SPRAY PAINTING

The key to spray painting is to hold the can about 12 inches from the object, and keep the can moving.

A

B

INTERNATIONAL KITCHEN

After eight years in their house, these homeowners haven't found the kitchen design that feels right. A global flavor to spice up the room is a perfect approach for these world travelers. They'll transform a boring, white kitchen into a bright space, playing off fun shades in their collection of tea boxes and a colorful souvenir from a trip.

BEFORE: This boring, white kitchen didn't represent the homeowner's international style.

◢ PROJECT SUMMARY ◣

With a little paint and creativity, this kitchen becomes an international café that reflects the homeowners' travels. There's a lot to work with – a utility table, pine table and chairs, a faux tile backboard, and cabinetry. The projects suggest different cultural influences — the tropics, Indonesia, and Mexico. Bold colors help add some worldly inspiration to an uninspiring room.

AFTER: The stenciled pattern on the cabinets lends an adventurous, Indonesian flavor to the room, while the hand-glazed tile pattern on the walls suggests the warmth of Mexico.

◢ CREATING WALL TILES ◣

Decorate the walls with a tile pattern that suggests a Mexican influence. The look of hand-glazed tile gives warmth and intimacy. The easy and fun glazing technique makes for a shiny finish. Start by washing the walls, covered with semi-gloss paint, to remove the sheen, grease, and dirt and to help the new paint stick.

You Will Need

Rosin paper	Small trays
1½" medium-tack painter's tape	3 quarts white primer
Trisodium phosphate	1 quart buff paint
Sponges	1 quart gray-green paint
Clean cloth	1 quart dark green paint
Dust brushes	Paper towels
Screwdrivers	2 quarts clear glaze
Bucket of water	Three 1-quart containers
⅛" blue auto-detailing tape	Spatulas
2" angle brushes	Three 4" rollers
6" rollers	2" foam brushes

1 Use the painter's tape to tape down the rosin paper to protect the floor (photo A). Tape off the cabinets and walls (photo B) to get clean, straight lines.

2 With the screwdrivers, remove the plates for switches and outlets. Mix one part trisodium phosphate to four parts warm water, and wash the walls with the clean cloth (photo C).

3 Tape off the top of the wall above the tile board. With the angle brush, cut in to apply the primer to the corners and edges (photo D), and with the 6" rollers, roll on the primer (photo E).

TIPS | DIY Network
Home Improvement

REMOVING SHEEN

Trisodium phosphate (TSP) removes the sheen, or protective surface, from old paint so new paint will stick. Sand any areas with loose or flaking paint before you apply trisodium phosphate.

4 Tape the grout lines with the auto-detailing tape (photo F). Mix one part of each color of paint with two parts of the clear glaze (photo G).

D

F

E

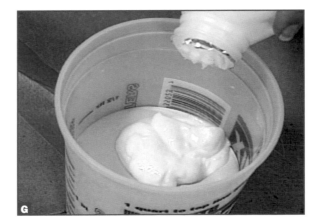

G

TIPS | DIY Network Home Improvement

FAUX TILE

Using two or more glaze colors at once creates variation in the depth of a surface. This finish creates the mottled look of hand-glazed tiles. This technique can be done on a regular wall, too, by adding the "grout" lines with narrow strips of tape.

5 With the 4" roller, randomly roll the first color on the wall to cover about 30 percent of the area (photo H). Then use the 4" rollers to fill in another 30 percent. Use the third color to fill in the rest of the area.

6 Fold the paper towels to form a smooth, fluffy pad, and spread the first color around the wall in big, circular motions (photo I). Work in small sections so the glaze doesn't dry. Get a fresh surface on the paper towels, and spread the second color. Finally, spread the third color and then wipe all three colors together, blending and softening them. Let the glazes dry.

7 After the glaze dries, tape along the bottom of the tile board trim to prepare it for a new glaze (photo J). With the foam brush, apply the dark green glaze. Use the paper towel technique to spread the glaze. Let it dry.

8 Remove the tape. With the angle brush, cut in with the varnish and then apply the varnish with the 6" rollers (photo K).

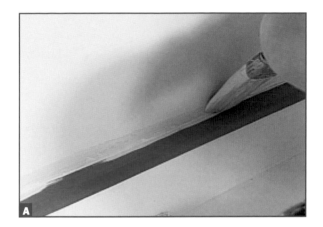

◄ PAINTING THE WALLS ►

The warm, sandy color ties in with the colors in a picture on the wall. The cozy shade is the perfect complement to the Mexican-themed tiles. You can use the roller extender to reach high spots without a ladder.

You Will Need

1½" medium-tack painter's tape	Extension roller
2" angle brushes	Trays
Large rollers	2 gallons of yellow matte finish

1 Tape off the trim. With the angle brushes, cut in (photo A).

2 Roll on the yellow paint (photo B). Use the extension roller to reach high places (photo C). Let it dry. Repeat if needed.

3 Pull off the tape at a 45-degree angle for a straight line (photo D).

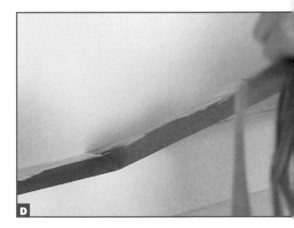

◀ STAINING THE TABLE AND CHAIRS ▶

The dark, teak-like stain on the furniture looks tropical and exotic and ties in with the warm wall color. Start by sanding the pieces with 150-grit sandpaper, which has a medium roughness. The lower the grit number, the coarser the paper. When applying the stain, remember that less is more. Keep spreading the stain until you use all the color on the brush. Using the foam brushes for the stain gives a more even coat with fewer brush marks.

You Will Need

150-grit sandpaper	1 pint latex stain in dark walnut
Medium sanding block	Small plastic containers
Dust brush	1" foam brushes
Tack cloth	2" foam brushes
Face mask	1 quart flat varnish

1 Wearing the face mask, sand the pieces with the sandpaper and sanding block (photo A).

2 With the sanding brush, clean the surfaces (photo B), and use the tack cloth to remove finer particles (photo C).

3 With both sizes of the foam brushes, apply the stain (photo D). Let it dry.

4 With both sizes of foam brushes, coat the pieces with the varnish for an older look.

STENCILING THE CABINETS

The homemade stencils, with a classic trellis pattern, give an adventurous Indonesian flavor to the room. When applying the paint, remember that a little paint goes a long way. A clover detail and an outline in paint add the finishing touches to the pattern.

You Will Need

Screwdrivers	Stippling brushes
Medium-size bucket with warm water	Paper towels
Sponges	6" flocked rollers
Clean cloths	Small trays
1" medium-tack painter's tape	1½" angle brushes
Posterboard stencils	Medium angled artist's brushes
1 quart dark brown eggshell finish paint	

1 With the screwdrivers, remove the cabinetry hardware. Clean the cabinets with warm, soapy water.

2 Create borders by taping the edges of each door and drawer with the blue tape. Tape the stencil to the cabinet (photo A).

3 Dip the stippling brush in a little bit of the dark brown paint (photo B), and dab the excess paint off on the paper towels (photo C).

TIPS | DIY Network Home Improvement

LATTICE PATTERN

You can buy lattice pattern stencils or create your own with ghosted grid posterboard, which can be found in some drug stores. The posterboard has a protective coat on one side with a grid pattern for guidance.

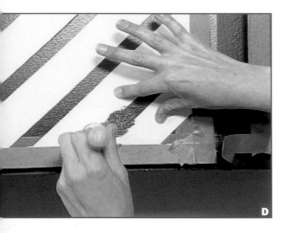

4 Hold down the area you're painting, and stipple, or dab, diagonal stripes on each surface with the posterboard stencil (photo D). Let it dry.

5 Turn the stencil over to create the crossing stripes, and stencil as you did before. Let it dry.

6 Place the clover stencil at staggered intersections and stipple (photo E).

7 With the artist's brush, add a thin outline to the pattern with the dark brown paint (photo F).

8 With the angle brush, cut in, and then use the flocked rollers to apply the varnish (photo G).

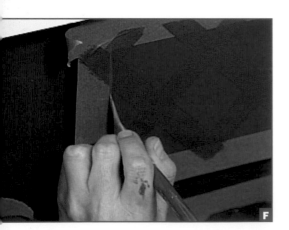

PAINTING THE UTILITY CART

Complete the cohesive design of this kitchen by making over the cart for a cozy and fun look. Use small brushes designed for tight, hard-to-reach spaces to get a better finish.

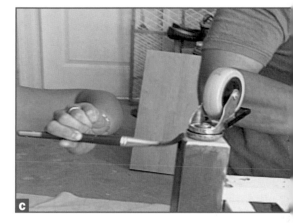

You Will Need	
Screwdriver	Different sizes of brushes to paint the cart's rack and legs
Cardboard	
1½" medium-tack painter's tape	1 quart navy blue semi-gloss

1 With the screwdriver, remove the cart's top (photo A). Put the cardboard beneath the cart so you can paint to the edge (photo B).

2 Tape off the surfaces that won't be painted. With the various brushes, apply the navy blue paint (photo C). Use a small artist's brush for corners (photo D).

4

Work & Play Rooms

As our lives get busier, we need some rooms to handle more than one function. We squeeze office space into our bedrooms and guest rooms and keep exercise equipment in our garages. Remember that the room's main function should receive primary attention while the extra activity should be assigned to a well-defined area. This keeps the room from feeling cluttered and unorganized. Similar colors and details will unify the activities, and separate, organized spaces will provide efficiency.

Shannon

GUEST COTTAGE

The 1970s-era home office, with wooden wall paneling and a dated wall unit, doesn't suit the homeowners' updated tastes. It's time to adapt the hodgepodge room with lots of space into a guest cottage by adding some color and coziness to the old-style furniture and cold, white walls.

◣ **PROJECT SUMMARY** ◢

A cottage theme pervades the room as the walls get some stripes, and the shelves are transformed to look rustic. The new walls make the room appear both bigger and cozier and help highlight the couple's collections of eclectic pieces. A makeover for the oak wall unit involves a traditional decorative painting technique to add texture, and the final touch is to paint some cool stools a splashy color.

y

z

q

w

e

r

t

u

i

o

p

a

BEFORE: The homeowner's small guest cottage was furnished with mismatched pieces that didn't work in their main house (above).

AFTER: Painting the walls and shelves in traditional colors and giving them a textured treatment gives the room a cohesive and vintage feel (top right, right, and below).

◀ PAINTING THE WALLS ▶

The new golden color warms up the sterile space. Paint in the panel seams, and add dash marks to give the feel of traditional cottage fabric. Using rollers with thicker than normal naps makes it easier to paint in the panel seams. Use extension rollers to reach the higher spots.

You Will Need

Floor cloth	4 ounces slate gray paint
1½" medium-tack painter's tape	Spatula
2 gallons golden matte	2" angle brushes
Small, angled artist's brushes	Paint mugs
Fluffy foam rollers	Paint can visor
Paint trays	Plastic bowl
Small, pointed artist's brushes	4 ounces navy blue paint

1 Cover the floor with the floor cloth, and tape it down. With the golden matte, use the angle brush to cut in (photo A).

2 With the roller, roll on one or two coats of paint in the rest of the room (photo B). Let it dry. With the small, angled artist's brushes, paint the panel seams navy blue using the seam line as a guide.

3 Count every three panels across the wall, and put a thin line of tape along the rolled stripes as a guide to make the dashes (photo C).

4 Use the tape as a guideline, and paint in the slate gray with the small, pointed artist's brush a dash about 1 inch long, skip an inch, and paint an inch along the edge of the tape (photo D). Repeat the pattern.

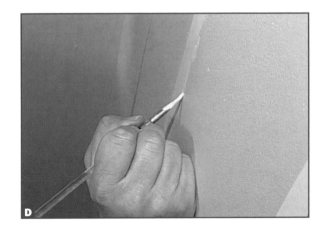

◀ PAINTING THE SHELVES ▶

A rust finish on the display shelves makes them appear heavier and rustic to fit the cottage theme. The base coat contains metal shavings that prompt rusting when you apply the rusting solution. A flat varnish protects the rust finish without making it look new.

You Will Need

Sandpaper block	4 ounces iron metallic surfacer
Dust brush	4 ounces rust antiquing solution
Tack cloth	1 quart flat varnish
Plastic bowl	3" foam brushes

1 Sand the surface so the paint will stick. Remove the grit with the brush and the tack cloth.

2 Brush on the metallic surfacer (photo A). After it dries, brush on the rusting solution (photo B). The more solution you apply, the more rusted the surface will become. Let it dry.

3 Brush on the flat varnish (photo C). Let it dry.

UPDATING THE WALL UNIT

First, paint the unit a gray-blue shade. Then add texture. This project uses the frottage technique, in which you brush on a glaze and then crumple newspaper and press it into the glaze to give a textured look. The more you press with the newspaper, the more you'll remove the glaze and reveal the color underneath.

A

You Will Need

Sandpaper	2 quarts primer tinted 50 percent to slate gray
Dust brush	2 quarts clear glaze
Tack cloth	2 quarts forest green eggshell paint
Painter's tape	Plastic container
2" square brushes	Stir stick
Cardboard	Couple of drops of universal tint in raw umber
Newspaper	

1 Sand the furniture to prepare it for painting. Then brush off the dust, and use the tack cloth to wipe away the residue. Tape off the areas where you don't want paint (photo A).

2 Put cardboard beneath the furniture so you can paint to the bottom of the piece (photo B).

3 With the square brush, apply the tinted primer over the whole piece inside and out, and let it dry. Brush on the forest green paint on the interior only. Let it dry (photo C).

B

TIPS | DIY Network
Home Improvement

TINTING
Universal tint is very concentrated; use just a small amount to get the desired effect when painting.

C

4 Mix one part of the forest green paint to two parts of the glaze. Brush on the tinted glaze one section at a time.

5 Crumple sheets of the newspaper, and press it gently into the glaze (photo D). Let it dry.

6 Add a couple drops of burnt umber tint to the flat varnish, stir the mixture, and apply the varnish (photo E). Let it dry.

◀ PAINTING THE STOOLS AND SIDE TABLE ▶

Change these seats and table from boring to bold with a lively red paint to spruce up the space with a cheerful look. These fun splashes of color help make the room feel like a retreat.

A

You Will Need

Sandpaper	1 quart barn red eggshell finish
Brush	Small square brushes
Tack cloth	Medium square brushes
1 quart slate gray primer	

1 Sand the stools and tabletop to prepare them for painting (photo A). Brush off the dust, and wipe away the residue with the tack cloth.

2 With the small square brushes, apply the same tinted primer you used on the wall unit. (photo B). Let it dry.

3 With random brush strokes, use the medium brushes to cover the pieces almost completely with the red paint (photo C).

B

C

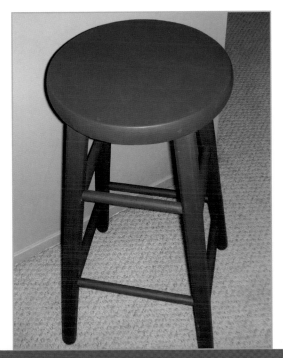

GARAGE PARTY ROOM

The stark, cold garage has an industrial feel with white walls and a concrete floor. The plan is to add some Hollywood glamour to the space by creating a snazzy lounge for watching movies and playing pool. The new party room will feature special effects and a silver screen in a spot reminiscent of a 1940's dance hall.

BEFORE: This homeowner wanted to turn the back end of her garage room into a game room, but didn't know how to bring this dingy, drab room to life.

◀ PROJECT SUMMARY ▶

Like creating a movie set, this room's transformation entails many aspects. Paint for the floor warms up the space. The focal point for the walls is a movie screen adorned with an art deco frame. The wine bar gets fresh paint and stencils with art deco details. The last step is to dress up decorative pots with spray paint and a glazed effect to add some style.

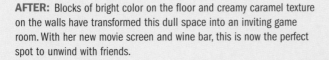

AFTER: Blocks of bright color on the floor and creamy caramel texture on the walls have transformed this dull space into an inviting game room. With her new movie screen and wine bar, this is now the perfect spot to unwind with friends.

A

B

C

PAINTING THE WALLS

Mix the warm caramel paint with the light molding paste, which is nonshrinking and covers screw holes. Make the mixing easier by using a drill with a paddle, then spread the mixture on the wall with the trowel. An important step is to tape off a rectangle for the movie screen.

You Will Need

Plastic dropcloths	Power drill
1½" medium-tack painter's tape	Mixing paddle
Duct tape	3 hawks, or metal palettes
Chalk line	2 French trowels (with rounded corners)
3 gallons molding paste	Paint trays
1 quart tan paint	Paint can visor

1 Prepare to paint by covering the cement floor with plastic tarps. Tape off the rectangle for the movie screen with the chalk line, and snap the line to get the dimensions you want (photo A).

2 Measure 3 gallons of molding paste and a ½ quart of paint, and mix them with the drill (photo B).

3 Put the plaster mixture on the hawk, and use the trowels to apply the mixture to the wall. First, trowel on the plaster in an arcing motion (photo C); then spread it down the wall, as if frosting a cake (photo D). Let it dry overnight.

D

CREATING THE MOVIE SCREEN

The center of the screen remains white to show movies. Paint a high-gloss black frame around the screen to add drama and decorate it with gold details for a real Hollywood look.

You Will Need

Tape measure	½"-1" artist's brushes
Level	1 quart high-gloss black paint
Pencils	8 ounces gold metallic paint
Small trays	Art deco stencil
2"-4" rollers	Stencil brushes

A

1 Measure 5¾ inches out from the tape all around the frame, and use the level to connect the dots (photo A). Tape off the new lines and paint the frame with the high-gloss black paint.

2 Dip the tips of the stenciling brushes into the gold paint, and blot off the extra paint.

3 Anchor the stencil on the frame with tape. Pounce the stencil with the brush to fill in the shapes and create the pattern (photo B).

B

TIPS | DIY Network Home Improvement

STENCIL VARIETY

Want to get creative? Craft stores carry stencils for many different designs, so choose one that works best for the theme of your room. Or try making your own with poster board and a craft knife.

PAINTING THE FLOORS

Create a sense of two rooms for a multipurpose hangout by painting the floor different colors in diagonal shapes. First, paint the floor brown, then add flair by painting a red section for films and an orange area for billiards.

You Will Need

Chalk line	3" angle brushes
1½" medium-tack painter's tape	Paint mugs
3 gallons dark brown patio paint	Varnish
Large paint trays	1 gallon brick red patio paint
Large rollers	1 gallon bright orange patio paint
Extension handles	

1 Sweep and mop the floor, and tape off the section to be painted. Paint the edges and corners with the angle brush (photo A).

2 Roll on the brown paint with the roller extension (photo B). Let it dry overnight.

3 Mark off the two diagonal sections and a border around the room with the pencil, and snap the chalk line to get the boundaries (photo C). Tape along the outside edge of the sections, and with the angle brush, apply varnish to the inside edge of the tape.

4 Use the rollers to paint the sections in red and orange. Let it dry, and apply a second coat if needed.

TIPS | DIY Network Home Improvement

CAUTION: WET PAINT

Floor paint is very durable, but make sure it cures properly with plenty of drying time before walking on it. Otherwise, you'll have to paint all over again.

◣ PAINTING THE WINE BAR ▣

This fun project livens up the furniture with black paint embellished by gold art deco-style details in stencils. Use foam brushes because they leave fewer brush marks. The result is a classic Hollywood look with a '40s-era theme.

You Will Need

Screwdriver	3" foam brushes
Sandpaper	1 quart of satin varnish
Dust brushes	Stippling brushes
Tack cloths	Adhesive stencil
1 quart black gesso	Burnishing tool
1 quart black matte paint	4 ounces gold metallic paint
2 small plastic containers	

1 Remove the hardware from the piece. Prepare to paint by sanding the furniture, brushing off the dust, and wiping away the residue with the tack cloth. Apply the black gesso with the foam brushes (photo A). Let it dry. Apply a solid coat of black paint.

2 Burnish the stencils by pressing the burnishing tool against the paper backing so the stencil pulls off easily (photo B).

3 Create a hinge with tape to keep the stencil in place while you remove the adhesive backing (photo C), then press out the stencil on the piece, burnish it again, and remove the backing.

A

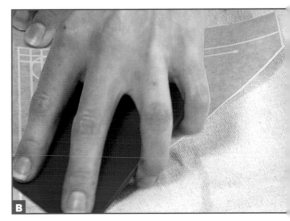

B

C

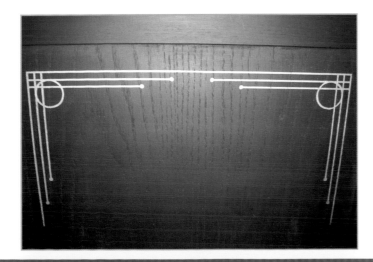

4 Place a piece of tape at the end of the stencil to have a stopping point. Pounce on the gold paint with quick jabs of the brush (photo D), and varnish the furniture with a foam brush to protect the piece (photo E).

◀ STIRRING UP THE POTS ▶

Embellishing these decorative planters with copper and bright blue spray paint adds jazz and style to the room. A glaze effect gives the pots more personality and livens up an already lively space.

You Will Need

Sandpaper	Hammered-copper spray paint
Tack cloth	Royal blue spray paint
Face mask	Dropcloth

1 Sand the pieces first so the paint will stick (photo A); then wipe away the residue with the tack cloth. Put on the face mask, and spray on the copper paint (photo B).

2 Spray the blue paint heavily on the pots so the paint drips and creates a glazed look (photo C). Be sure to wear the face mask.

ROMANTIC AFRICAN STUDY

The homeowner's mission is to transform a boring, uninspiring office into a warm, inviting space in which to work. The secret is soft, serene, comforting colors with an exotic look, reminiscent of Africa, to play off the animal-influenced décor. The result is a stylish and cozy space with worldly sophistication.

BEFORE: This home office had all the makings of an efficient workspace, but the homeowner rarely spent time there. In order to make the space an appealing place to spend time, inspiration was drawn from the room's existing artwork.

◣ **PROJECT SUMMARY** ◢

The walls and ceiling get a new coat of earthy tan and beige tones. The built-in shelves remain white, but an elephant-hide texture on the back of the shelves adds drama and elegance. Create an exciting focal point by decoupaging the side table with a world map on top and then painting the piece to give rustic warmth. A garishly green lamp has a makeover with some cool black paint and details.

AFTER: An inviting new color on the walls, textured shelves, and a makeover for the table lamp transform the space into a warm inviting space to work.

◢ PAINTING THE WALLS AND CEILING ◣

The aim is to change the bland walls into a look of romantic Africa. The neutral colors give drama to the room but still convey softness and sophistication. Paint the ceiling first to make cleaning up easier.

You Will Need

Sponges	Large rollers
Bucket of warm water	Roller extension
Dropcloths	Trays
1½" medium-tack painter's tape	2" angle brushes
1 quart varnish	1 gallon taupe matte finish paint
Medium artist's brushes	1 gallon brown matte finish paint

1 With the sponges, wash the baseboards, door jambs, and other trim. Put the painter's tape around all of the trim and built-in shelves (photo A). Lay down the dropcloths.

2 With the artist's brush, spread a small amount of varnish along the edges of the tape to get clean paint lines (photo B).

3 With the angle brush, cut in around the ceiling's edges with the taupe paint (photo C). With the extension roller, fill in the ceiling (photo D), and let it dry. Repeat if needed.

4 Cut in on the edges around the walls with the brown paint. With the extension rollers, roll the paint on the walls (photo E). Let it dry, and repeat if needed. Remove the tape.

TIPS | DIY Network
Home Improvement

PAINTED CEILINGS

Color on a ceiling creates drama
and warmth. To avoid too dark ceilings when painting, use a tone that's
a few shades lighter than the wall
color. For a more dramatic effect,
make a canopy with the same color
on the walls and ceiling.

◣ ADDING TEXTURE TO THE BUILT-IN SHELVES ◥

Create a cool visual effect — and give a sense of safari — by adding texture to the back walls of the shelves. To do this, press cheesecloth against wet glaze and push the fabric's texture into the wall with rollers.

You Will Need

1½" medium-tack painter's tape	Several yards cheesecloth
Face masks	6" dry roller
150-grit sandpaper	1½" angle brushes
Tack cloth	4" rollers
1 quart clear glaze	Medium artist's brushes
1 quart clear varnish	Trays
1 quart pale pink eggshell paint	Plastic container
Sample size gray paint	Spatula
1 quart primer tinted to pale pink paint	

1 Tape off the back panels. Sand the panels and use the tack cloth to remove the finer dust particles (photo A).

2 With the artist's brushes, seal the tape with clear varnish (photo B), and let it dry.

3 With the angle brush, cut in on the edges with the primer (photo C). With the 4" roller, fill in the rest of the panels with the primer (photo D). Let it dry. Repeat the steps using the pink paint.

TIPS | DIY Network Home Improvement

PAINTING SHELVES

If the shelves are painted in oil paint, use an oil-based primer for the best adhesion. Water-based paints work best with water-based primer.

4 Mix two parts of the clear glaze with one part of the gray paint (photo E). Cut in, and roll on the glaze mixture with the 4" rollers.

5 Push the cheesecloth, slightly rumpled, into the wet glaze (photo F). Use the 6" dry roller to press the texture against the wall (photo G).

6 Remove the cloth, and let it dry well. Touch up any areas that didn't texture well by blotting them with the cheesecloth (photo H).

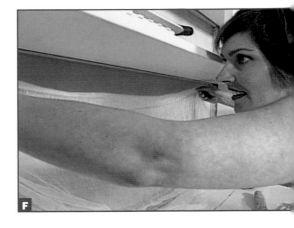

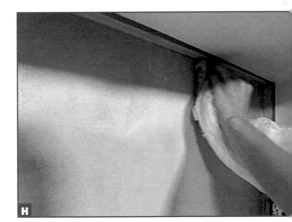

◀ DECOUPAGING THE TABLE ▶

Liven up the side table with worldly flair from a map of Africa. Some spray from a water bottle adds a distressed look for some worldly sophistication.

You Will Need

Face masks	1 quart primer tinted to beige
Foam sanders	1 quart beige
Tack cloth	Couple of drops of universal tint in raw umber
Cardboard	Plastic spreader
Matte medium	Spray bottle
Map of Africa	Small container of water
1 quart satin varnish	Six 3" foam brushes
2½" dry square brushes	

1 Wearing the face mask, sand the table with the foam sanders (photo A). Wipe away the dust with the tack cloth. Put cardboard under the table legs (photo B).

2 With the foam brushes, apply the tinted primer (photo C), and let it dry. With the foam brushes, apply a coat of the beige paint, and let it dry.

TIPS | DIY Network Home Improvement

GO WITH THE GRAIN

To hide brush marks, brush against the grain for good coverage, then brush with the grain in light, even strokes.

3 Brush the back of the map with the matte medium (photo D), and brush the tabletop with the matte medium (photo E).

4 While the tabletop is wet, place the map on the table, and use the spreader to smooth out air pockets (photo F). Let it dry.

5 Brush the top of the table with the matte medium to seal the map (photo G), and let it dry.

6 Tint the varnish with the universal tint, and brush the varnish on the tabletop (photo H).

7 While the varnish is wet, spray water on the surface (photo I). Let it set for a minute, and then blend it with the dry square brush (photo J). Repeat the process on the table legs, and let it dry.

PAINTING THE LAMP

Black paint and brass details transform this funky lamp into a sleek, stylish piece. Shake the spray paint can for about a minute before use, then hold the can about a foot from the surface, and keep it moving.

You Will Need

- Paper towels
- Dropcloth
- 1½" medium-tack painter's tape
- Face masks
- Black spray paint
- 4 ounces bronze acrylic paint
- Small artist's brushes

1 Remove the lampshade, lightbulbs, and harp. Fill the outlet with paper towels.

2 Tape off the brass stem and chord (photo A). Wearing the mask, spray the paint on the base (photo B). Let it dry, and spray another coat if needed.

3 Tape off sections of the base and lampshade before you add the detail (photo C).

4 With the artist's brush, apply the bronze acrylic paint to the base and shade in your choice of details (photo D). Remove the tape.

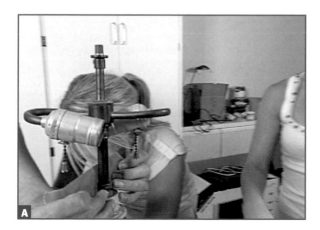

A

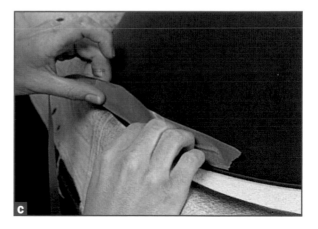

C

B

D

Index

METRIC CONVERSION TABLE

Inches	Decimal Inches	Rounded Metric	Inches	Decimal Inches	Rounded Metric	Inches	Decimal Inches	Rounded Metric
1/16	.0625	1.6 mm/.16 cm	7½	7.5	19 cm	18		45.7 cm
1/8	.0125	3 mm/.3 cm	7¾	7.75	19.7 cm	18¼	18.25	46.4 cm
3/16	.1875	5 mm/.5 cm	8		20.3 cm	18½	18.5	47 cm
¼	.25	6 mm/.6 cm	8¼	8.25	21 cm	18¾	18.75	47.6 cm
5/16	.3125	8 mm/.8 cm	8½	8.5	21.6 cm	19		48.3 cm
3/8	.375	9.5 mm/.95 cm	8¾	8.75	22.2 cm	19¼	19.25	48.9 cm
7/16	.4375	1.1 cm	9		22.9 cm	19½	19.5	49.5 cm
½	.5	1.3 cm	9¼	9.25	23.5 cm	19¾	19.75	50.2 cm
9/16	.5625	1.4 cm	9½	9.5	24.1 cm	20		50.8 cm
5/8	.625	1.6 cm	9¾	9.75	24.8 cm	20¼	20.25	51.4 cm
11/16	.6875	1.7 cm	10		25.4 cm	20½	20.5	52.1 cm
¾	.75	1.9 cm	10¼	10.25	26 cm	20¾	20.75	52.7 cm
13/16	.8125	2.1 cm	10½	10.5	26.7 cm	21		53.3 cm
7/8	.875	2.2 cm	10¾	10.75	27.3 cm	21¼	21.25	54 cm
15/16	.9375	2.4 cm	11		27.9 cm	21½	21.5	54.6 cm
			11¼	11.25	28.6 cm	21¾	21.75	55.2 cm
1		2.5 cm	11½	11.5	29.2 cm	22		55.9 cm
1¼	1.25	3.2 cm	11¾	11.75	30 cm	22¼	22.25	56.5 cm
1½	1.5	3.8 cm	12		30.5 cm	22½	22.5	57.2 cm
1¾	1.75	4.4 cm	12¼	12.25	31.1 cm	22¾	22.75	57.8 cm
2		5 cm	12½	12.5	31.8 cm	23		58.4 cm
2¼	2.25	5.7 cm	12¾	12.75	32.4 cm	23¼	23.25	59 cm
2½	2.5	6.4 cm	13		33 cm	23½	23.5	59.7 cm
2¾	2.75	7 cm	13¼	13.25	33.7 cm	23¾	23.75	60.3 cm
3		7.6 cm	13½	13.5	34.3 cm	24		61 cm
3¼	3.25	8.3 cm	13¾	13.75	35 cm	24¼	24.25	61.6 cm
3½	3.5	8.9 cm	14		35.6 cm	24½	24.5	62.2 cm
3¾	3.75	9.5 cm	14¼	14.25	36.2 cm	24¾	24.75	62.9 cm
4		10.2 cm	14½	14.5	36.8 cm	25		63.5 cm
4¼	4.25	10.8 cm	14¾	14.75	37.5 cm	25¼	25.25	64.1 cm
4½	4.5	11.4 cm	15		38.1 cm	25½	25.5	64.8 cm
4¾	4.75	12 cm	15¼	15.25	38.7 cm	25¾	25.75	65.4 cm
5		12.7 cm	15½	15.5	39.4 cm	26		66 cm
5¼	5.25	13.3 cm	15¾	15.75	40 cm	26¼	26.25	66.7 cm
5½	5.5	14 cm	16		40.6 cm	26½	26.5	67.3 cm
5¾	5.75	14.6 cm	16¼	16.25	41.3 cm	26¾	26.75	68 cm
6		15.2 cm	16½	16.5	41.9 cm	27		68.6 cm
6¼	6.25	15.9 cm	16¾	16.75	42.5 cm	27¼	27.25	69.2 cm
6½	6.5	16.5 cm	17		43.2 cm	27½	27.5	69.9 cm
6¾	6.75	17.1 cm	17¼	17.25	43.8 cm	27¾	27.75	70.5 cm
7		17.8 cm	17½	17.5	44.5 cm	28		71.1 cm
7¼	7.25	18.4 cm	17¾	17.75	45.1 cm			